Waiting for an Answer

Heather Sullivan

Nixes Mate Books
Allston, Massachusetts

Copyright © 2017 Heather Sullivan

Book design by d'Entremont
Cover found photograph and art by Lauren Leja

All rights reserved. This book or any portion thereof may not be reproduced or used in any manner whatsoever without the express written permission of the publisher except for the use of brief quotations in a book review or scholarly journal.

Thanks to Michael McInnis, Anne Pluto, Lauren Leja, John Dorsey, Rebecca Schumedja, Michael Hathaway, and Pressure Press Presents. Thanks to Rusty Barnes, my first reader, Sierra, Rider & Logan Barnes, my hope, joy, and happiness, and Laurel Sullivan. I'm still waiting.

ISBN 978-0-9991882-0-0

Nixes Mate Books
POBox 1179
Allston, MA 02134
nixesmate.pub/books

*For him, for them and for her.
It's always been for her.*

Contents

Number Four	1
Tea	2
This Line Here	4
Toronto	5
Tent	6
Stage Left	8
Slicing	10
Atlantic Line	11
Green Beans	12
Waiting for an Answer	14
Her Regard	16
Control	18
Fan	19
Sweet Potato	20
Blockade	22
Erin	24
Immortal	25
Pain Management	26
Letters	28
Channel	29
Radioactive	30

Petunias	31
Worn out	32
Red Hot	34
Repose	35
Tremulous	36
Earthquake	38
Dervish	39
Station Wagon	40
Tuning	42
Canvas	43
Where You Came From	44
Bolt	46
Superstition	47
What She Said	48
Mural	49
Ode to George Eliot	50
Times Three	51
In My Cups	52
One-Two	54
Ticks	55

Waiting for an Answer

Number Four

I still talk about you even though
I never gave you a name,

feeling that if I had taken that leap
forward I might have been left

suspended in mid-air like Wile E. Coyote,
except release arrived for him when

skull met canyon floor, and for me
there would be no absolution.

I would hang there, pinioning wildly,
clawing for ledge or outstretched root,

something to help gain purchase.
Nameless you remain for my sanity, but

your place in the lineage cemented
nonetheless. Coming home from work,

your shadow joins them when
they greet me at the front door.

Tea

The lake at the Tobyhanna Army Depot had
a small manmade beach front that we went

to on sunny weekends, which was as close as
mom could get to a relaxing body of water in

the Poconos. We were hours away from the
ocean with a car that didn't go in reverse, so

we made do with what we had. There was a
cordoned off area for the little kids, and one

lifeguard on duty. When he took a break or
called out sick, they put up a sign telling you

that you were on your own. The silty water
made you look like a used tea bag when you

emerged from its depths, sometimes with a
lily pad or funky line of algae stuck to the back

of your leg or your swimsuit. There was a
concession stand where the kids with money

could get soft serve ice cream in a waffle cone.
We knew not to ask, instead we would pull out

a PB&J sandwich from the blue Coleman cooler
that travelled with us from state to state and long

ago sat in the true sand of California, staring out
on ocean waves so perfect they will haunt your

visions now when you go to the attic to get a
box fan and gently move that cooler to the right.

This Line Here

Imaginary boundary lines are set up,
as value systems are formed,
consciousness creating markers of our absolutes.
Transitioning with time and circumstance,
if he lies to me,
if he breaks my heart,
if he cheats on me.
You and I used to say,
at least he doesn't hit me.
High water marks these,
the daily issues safely floating underneath
the margin of error.

There was a little girl with Holly Hobby curtains,
knee socks that she rolled down to her ankles,
always afraid of drowning.

Toronto

It was a small café,
tucked into a side street
on the way to a castle,
that my grandfather told us
we had to see.
Still learning each other's ins and outs,
it was our first trip together.
Hot chocolate and croissants,
we played at being grown-ups in this foreign city.

One slightly outdated map and challenging hike later,
we stumbled onto the landmark.
Expecting a castle,
we got a huge mansion built by a wealthy man for
the woman he loved.
We explored the hidden passageways,
marveled at the furnishings.
Standing on an upper outside balcony,
I leaned over the edge knowing it would
drive you crazy.
Knowing you would grab me and pull me close.

I still lean out over every edge I can find.

Tent

From a distance, the tent caterpillars in my mother's
backyard, made the trees appear to have webbed

flesh from limb to limb, some ghostly attempt at
colossal hands rising up from the ground. On closer

inspection, the ripples from the pupa working their
way out were difficult to stop staring at, not quite as

adorable as the chicks in the warmer at the county
fair, but equally struggling at rebirth. I understood

that primal desire to strike out then, knowing that
the required separation would be tiring. Now I spin

my own silk nightly, making pass after pass with warp
and weft in patterns that would make Arachne cross

her arms in satisfaction. I would bind mine in duct
tape, give them nuts and seeds to chew so their teeth

would dull, making it impossible to work their way out from the cocoon and away from me. I would coo in

their ears trying to forestall the inevitable hunt for their own cherry or birch tree, trying to keep them home.

Stage Left

I was nine years old when we went
to the circus in Cincinnati.
On the trip there,
you reminded us about The Who concert
only two years earlier
where eleven people had died after
being crushed to death against
the entrance doors.
I kept scanning the auditorium for the exits.
I think that trip is the origin
of my need to find the signs,
to plan the escape route
at the movie theatre,
re-read the flotation directions
as we sit on the tarmac.
While the motorcycle act circled around
inside the giant steel orb,
narrowly missing each other
on every turn,
I kept my fingers crossed as a talisman.
You bought us a program to share,
a tiger balloon for me,

pinwheel for my sister,
a plastic snake that undulated
when my brother held the tail.
Safely out in the night air,
each breath I took was for
a dozen lungs.

Slicing

Like a Sunday morning poached egg, my edges
are frayed, uneven, requiring a trim from the

scissors housed on the magnetic strip beside
the stove, below the mildly dull chef knives of

varying lengths. I slapped a serrated blade into
place with too much vigor and watched its peer

drop to the floor beside my foot, narrowly
missing the chance to send little pig to market.

We slice strips from our calves and wrists, turning
into trembling marionettes, walking en pointe

from room to room in search of eyeglasses still
perched on heads like coffee cups left on car roofs

on the way to work, or hunt for where we left the
phone, electronic teat to our mother's milk data plan.

The anti-lotus in the corner, folded in on ourselves,
no escaping the gravitational pull of this black hole.

Atlantic Line

There was three inch thick ice
trapped under the snow,
blocking the backed up rain water
from the sewer grate,
so we stood like railroad men swinging
alternating hammers at the spike,
armed instead with snow shovels and
garden tools chipping away a
millimeter with each arc.
Eventually the dam was breached,
and we used the broad flat shovels
to paddle our paper sailing ships
out onto the open water,
past the lobster boats and yellow slickers,
till darkness joined the sounds
of humpback whales.

Green Beans

From the outside everything looked
lovely, but the oven didn't work and

all the windows were painted shut.
It was stifling in the summer. We

weren't supposed to mention any of
it to the landlord, because you were

afraid he'd raise the rent and kick us
out. Be glad you have a roof over your

head. We weren't supposed to talk to
anyone else either, because you don't

air dirty laundry in public. You put a
toaster oven on the back left burner,

If it didn't fit, we didn't eat it. As simple
as that. I learned how to make green

bean casserole and date nut bread in
very small pans. You decorated with

Salvation Army store finds, painted
designs on repurposed furniture, like

setting the dining room tables on the
Titanic. I soaked up your teachings,

learned to keep my own counsel,
dress a pretty corpse to keep the

tenant quiet until the rent check clears.

Waiting for an Answer

When you put your ear
up to the hollowed out
cavity where my good
humors used to live, can
you hear the ache and
grind of frozen gears,
teeth matted together
with hairballs and out of
shape dust bunnies, more
grand echo then call and
response, feet planted on
the edge of the big, black
void, dropping pansies like
depth charges to locate the
bottom. In the back of your
throat, the tell-tale clacking
of bamboo knitting needles
purling a shroud for every
day wear that's reversible
for a night out, keeps away
the chill but makes it difficult
to get a word in edgewise.

A warm shower, spine curled
at the drain, with the water
muffling your lowing will
loosen your tongue.

Her Regard

I used to chase the sun, laying on the beach
next to my mother in her snakeskin patterned

swimsuit, reading novels about poets being
haunted by succubi, shaking my fist at passing

clouds. I would slather on the baby oil knowing
that first I would look like a beet but later on more

akin to a cream puff left in the oven just a tick too
long. No pain, no gain. But then in my freshman

year, she sent a clipping from a women's magazine
which informed me that one bad sunburn in your

life made you 250% more likely to develop skin
cancer. Starting to count, I ran out of fingers, toes

and multiple passing by appendages, before I
decided the point had been made. From then on,

floppy hats, SPF in my morning cereal, walking in
the shadows and courting translucence. I tell

myself that men prefer pale over golden brown,
while I seek out another poet to enthrall.

Control

The constant controlling of the public
and private faces seems to be like

the balance beam in junior high gym class,
struggling to put one foot in front of

the other while trying to keep your
shorts from riding up your thighs.

It's a tiring illusion.
Harder still to reconcile the appetite

to hand it all over to you when your
breath skims my cheek in the dark.

Fan

Sitting in front of the box fan, I watch the cat hair
swirl around the floor and the gnats bounce off

me that have gotten sucked through the holes in
the window screen. An occasional moth appears

out of nowhere, driving the cats to the back of the
couch and up the wall, until the heat wins out and

they retreat to the ground, stretch themselves
against the tile, looking for a cool spot, while the

moth now dances a tantalizing fuck you jig just
beyond their reach. Every time a hair grazes my

shoulder, instinct screams bug and pushes me to look,
while logic reminds me of the air currents and keeps

me still. Just like at work today when I was alone, and
it felt like someone brushed the back of my head. Logic

ran the potential answers, while instinct mouthed
your name. I held my breath hoping you'd do it again.

Sweet Potato

I call you my cherry blossom, my turtledove, my
sweet potato pie. The last one thanks in large part

to your red hair, so bright it's almost orange.
Random strangers have commented during the

entirety of your life on how pretty the color, how
all the little girl's hearts will be broken one day.

You always say thank you, gently rolling your eyes
when they leave. I kept it long when you were tiny,

not having the strength to force you into the societal
construct the other little boys in the apartment

complex pursued. Now that the choice is yours, you
have followed suit. We were having dinner at a

local steak house when you were four. Tommy
Lasorda walked through the door, glad handing the

diners, one by one. At our table, he told your father how lucky he was to be seated with three pretty girls,

a wife and two daughters. You looked him in the eye indignantly, "I'm not a girl just because I have long

hair." Not impressed, you went back to your macaroni and cheese, and he turned tail.

Blockade

My father took two things very seriously,
the Navy and the South. As children, we
learned to admire the immaculate dress

whites under the dry cleaning bag plastic,
but to never touch. We were respectful to
his crazy mother, the grandmother who

sent our Christmas checks taped to her
church program, each highlighted paragraph
a not so subtle clue to our inequities. After

their divorce, Mom used to say that her
genes cancelled his out, and so we stopped
talking about half our history, pretending

instead that we sprang from her thigh, the
distance from him making it easier to outrun
his anger. To discuss missing lineage now is

akin to sitting in the bathroom with the door
blocked, looking at the vintage Playboys he
used to hide in the bottom of his t-shirt

drawer. We whisper about Meade County,
Kentucky and Ireland before that, what it means
to be Southern and if we're even allowed to

pretend. To acknowledge the other half of the
whole, means bearing witness to the complete
picture. You can't play at confederacy without

feeling his hard hands just at the edge of your
shoulders, the fear rising from your stomach,
knowing that you are capable of terrible things.

Erin

She is Broadway show tunes
and digging in the dirt
to plant mountain laurel with her
bare hands.
She is home cooked lamb chops
and my first and only Rancid t-shirt.
She is sensible work clothes
from Lands' End and intricate tattoos
that wind around her porcelain skin.
She is perfectly coifed hair,
makeup wipes in her purse
and the proper conjugation of fuck.
She is the definition of generosity.
She is sitting stock still,
holding the hand of a veteran who
in a moment of clarity from the voices
realizes he is dying.
She is timely paperwork filled out in
triplicate with the goldenrod copy
going to right the office
and crying in the car where
no one can see.

Immortal

I spun at Woodstock,
untying mud smeared flesh in
swirls of colored sound,
each widening sphere,
loosening the hold of hem and haw.

Swimming in vapor,
my words held power,
Pythia,
hair on end,
this ecstasy.

Priestess of Athena,
I submit to the weaving,
take the warp and weft,
lay my body on the loom.

At last,
the moon calls,
strapping on sandals,
my terrifying radiance,
Inanna,
untiring,
we dance.

Pain Management

The measurement of pain is so subjective,
your three might be my seven. It's hard

to pretend to be an adult when the nurse lady
asks you to point to which of the increasingly

disappointed smiley faces you currently sit at.
Tell me baby, how bad is your ouchey?

You smile, begrudgingly point to the
straight line; she shakes her head in imagined

understanding and then tells you to take
more Tylenol, get some rest, try ice or heat.

What you want to say is give me the good stuff,
codeine, morphine, IV drip, anything to make

me feel human and viable again. Please help
me remember what normal feels like, or

to remember what it is to not feel anything.
I've been dying every day since she left, losing

more of my grip on the proper decorum that's
supposed to accompany these responses.

Letters

You're lying on your stomach on the couch,
legs bent, ankles crossed, face inches from

the notebook in front of your eyes, holding
fast your father's special black ink pen.

This practice of sounding out the letters one
by one, first forming words into thoughts

then into ideas that will propel your feet and
mind towards the inescapable future, where

I will not be. It starts innocently enough with
A is for apple, picking up speed with each new

symbol of freedom, until you can reach the
upper cabinets without your stepstool, have

conversations with me about your period and
how to properly put on eyeliner. The blink

completes with the flash of your ponytail
swinging up on your way out the front door.

Channel

There's an itchy spot on the side of my ankle
that I sometimes mindlessly scratch, and then
drift off to a foreign place where the kids are
still little and the improbable is within reach.
I can see them in their pajamas, standing
side by side, brushing their teeth in the doorway
of the bathroom in our tiny third floor walkup.
They're grinning and dancing, hopping from foot
to foot. I've told them to be careful, but
I'm only half serious and they know it.
My sister takes a picture, and later they frame
this moment for me in popsicle sticks and feathers.
A frozen instant, where her shoulder peeks out
from her too-big nightdress and he holds his
spider-man pose for the camera. I would
scratch a channel through my leg to stay here.

Radioactive

While lying on the scanner table,
I watch my kidneys function
on the monitor over my head.
A radioactive tracer gradually fills
in the image of two pale sisters
dancing in my abdomen, forever
tethered at the waist. My bladder
becomes as obvious as the tension
in my voice when asked whether
there's any chance I'm pregnant.
In another time, I watched the side
of a face appear, nose and chin,
rounded cheek. Now, I measure
each breath while the table bites
into my lower back. The technician
is methodical while shielding herself
from the radiation, answers every
question about the process. It's only
later in the parking garage, the same
level I was on the day mom died,
that I realize for over an hour there
was no buffer for the tender sisters,
chained in place becoming ever
more tired from the dance.

Petunias

I will dig in the dirt of your grave with my hands,
trowel forgotten in the trunk of our rental car,
plant the three roadside nursery petunias that
we will have picked out minutes earlier,
not knowing whether or not the groundskeeper
will mow them flush with the earth after our ritual.
With the pads of my fingers I will rub the
asparagus colored moss from your gravestone,
your sister's,
your father's,
your grandparent's.
I will touch the unmarked spot of your mother,
promise her again that when the time is right,
I will buy her a stone that I can tend to every year,
mark with flowers and tears,
as I do yours.
Hoping that my words reach you on the
wings of the mosquitos that surround me,
the blood sacrifice given in payment for their
whispered weight.

Worn out

The despondent slough is difficult
to escape, like all those quicksand
pits the TV shows in the 80's were
constantly prepping us for, but
much like removing home economics
from middle school means nobody
can balance a checkbook anymore,
failing to keep up with those PSA's
the A-Team provided weekly means
I'm thigh deep in despair, and I can't
find anybody with a handy vine.
Worn out and shaken dry, I'm like a
toner cartridge that you're trying to
coax one more desperate copy from,
that resume that will mean all the
difference, or a poem to win her back,
the suicide note that clears it all up,
that tax extension due tomorrow, a
form in triplicate cut in half. I write
of guilt and sin, the tragedy of lost
moments with children that will never
be relived, your husband's missed

birthday thanks to another late night
at the office, unspoken reassurances
to a dead mother. Fully awake in the
mire and alert to my lost condition,
apprehensions settle around my
waist like a training belt squeezing
those floating ribs up into my throat,
coalescing into a lump that can't be
swallowed, but I'm not known for my
fashion sense so it's more like the haute
couture version of a hair shirt, penance
for things I couldn't control but some-
how should have known to predict.

Red Hot

When in college with a few extra dollars,
we would eat at a hole-in-the-wall
sandwich shop that served turkey subs
the way you liked,
a basket of fries to share.
We'd sword fight with the red sandwich picks.
You would wipe your face with
a napkin from the dispenser,
wrapping it around the previous one,
forming a ball that you would try to tuck
off to the side.
I would tease you for the mess you made.
A man makes love the way he eats, I said.
You liked that idea,
getting into the thick of it,
like the way you would take an atomic fireball candy
and crunch it between your back molars,
refusing to wait for your reward,
only a root canal brought that to a halt.

Repose

Talk to me about the poetry you
love and whether a troubled soul
makes a better writer, put your
head in my lap and let me stroke
your hair while you rest. I will run
the knuckle of my index finger up
and down your cheek, and dream
of long, cool evenings spent twined
together with only a sheet between
my thighs, your hand on my belly.
We run hot, you and I, no need for
anything more. In the morning, I
will slip away, bring back coffee and
pastries, while the eggs simmer next
to home fries. Soft and silent, your
hands on my hips will pull me close,
and turning the stove off, I know I
will go wherever you take me.

Tremulous

The first time I felt the earth move was at a
gas station in San Diego, CA in the late 1970's.

My mom had the pump nozzle in her hand
and was stilled in mid-process. She stood there

surfing the tremor. After it passed, we were
on our way, my siblings and I vibrating on high.

We had experienced an earthquake and lived
to tell the tale. The next fifty times of upheaval

came with each backhand he would deliver to
her face while in front of us, like the ripping sound

of the needle on my Fisher Price record player
skidding across one of her 45's, the perfect union

of Marvin Gaye and Tammi Terrell silenced.
My grandfather taught me how to walk noiselessly

through the woods, watching out for dry leaves
and twigs that would alert those around me to

my presence. He said this was how the Indians
did it, how they hunted and survived, how if you

stood still long enough, you could become rooted to
one spot and watch the world carry on without you.

Earthquake

I feel the earth move when I finish the last glass
of wine in the bottle, trying to make my way to

the bathroom, the wall comes up fast on my right.
Striving to steady myself with my hand, it's easier

to lean into my entire arm, roll up into the shoulder
and then slide the rest of the way to the corner.

After I wash my hands, I'm just glad the kids are
asleep. Glad I am alone to watch shitty television

and pine after lost loves, lost choices, a lost mother.
What I am and what I should be are two totally

different things. What I do and what I am are two
totally different things. The job description does

not match what we went over in training. I'm just
waiting for my review to weigh my options.

Dervish

Rolling end to end on the couch,
you are electrified with static,
hair dancing in circles around your head
like Sufis in unending spirals,
memories of playing skin the cat
on the playground
until nausea overtook me.
You scuff your socks on the rug,
akin to Ali in the ring,
touch your ungrounded siblings
over and over to watch the spark
leap from your finger.
In this time of matter and mass,
you dance across the pinhead,
immaterial spirit made visible.

Station Wagon

She made us hand sewn burlap travel bags
both to keep our little minds occupied

on the car trip from California to Kentucky,
the land of our father's people, and to

keep us out of his hair. She filled them
with coloring books and crayons, Hot

Wheels, puzzle books, a soft toy for the
baby. She had collected and saved for

months, painted our names on one side
and a picture on the other. Mine was a tiger

emerging from a kaleidoscope forest. Her
talent played out before a limited crowd,

although she always signed every piece of
her art in the corner, a small act of rebellion.

All our money for the trip was bundled in
a tin Band-Aid box, long before credit cards

and ATM's were on every corner. Somewhere
in the Southwest, we spent the night in a

roadside motel with the loot hidden under
the bed. The next day we were an hour away,

when Mom realized the money had been left
behind. We raced his rising anger all the way

back, to learn there was still honesty left in
this world when the manager handed it over.

Outside, he hit her nonetheless, and then we
learned that no good deed goes unpunished.

Tuning

Running through the house naked
after your shower,
you flash past me and land with a thud
in front of the box fan
by the back door directing the hope
of a cool breeze inward,
cross-legged,
your little body takes the shape of a viola.
Ululating into the grate,
the pitch goes higher and higher,
as though you are summoning
humpback whales to come into the harbor.
The cats leave the room,
sensing the impending doom brought on
by unwelcome marine mammals.

Canvas

I am painted in invisible ink, a bowl
of lemon juice always at the ready,
the proofing flame makes each pretty
picture visible from the inside, passion
plays showing in sepia every night
of the week with a matinee on Sundays.
The names of lovers inked in the creases
of my hips and ringing my waist, like a
low slung bandolier riding my thighs,
each casing holding an unanswered shot
across the bow between you and I.
Childhood plays behind my throat,
ancestry on the small of my back.
The children measure their height against
my spine, while our story plays out like
Koi chasing the moon on my arms. I
swallowed the brush, so she could mark
the interior, turn me to stone, the discovery
akin to Lascaux, but no mold to slow the
arrow as it breaks my heart.

Where You Came From

There's this pier near the house where
I walk after the last dish is washed.
Past each unknown neighbor,
shades drawn day and night,
one old Italian guy on the stoop with a cigar,
head nod exchanged,
past the recycling bins out regardless
of the day of the week,
flashed glimpse of a skunk tucking
under the lattice work of the porch
on that big Victorian house perpetually
under construction.
Round the corner at the bottom of the hill,
cross under the streetlight
and onto the wooden planking,
enter a thousand moons ago when
the ocean smelled differently and
the flowers came in hues
I can't find anymore,
watch the roil, hear the crash
sound like a call and response echo
to a childhood that is long gone and

murky below the whitecaps,
before heading home to the constant.
Sometimes you have to drink
the water where you came from.

Bolt

The thunderstorm forced us from the highway,
the exit ramp leading to a mall lot.
We parked to wait it out,
just as lightning struck the concrete five feet away.
Fearing it would hit the car,
you commanded us out and
into the rain towards the building,
one child in your arms and another clutching at your shirt.
The eldest ran between us,
looking back to see if I would be washed away,
the gap expanding.
Maybe Lot's wife turned back not to get
one more look at her home,
but to judge the distance for her daughter's safety,
to ensure the fire would nip her heels first,
laying down the trench to protect the future.

Superstition

She promised on scout's honor,
even though she really didn't understand
what that meant,
only the knowing solemnity in
her father's eyes when he would
speak the words,
the sense of enormity.
When I was in elementary school,
we would cross our hearts and
hope to die,
stick a needle in our eye and
eat a frog alive.
Some would swear on their mother's graves,
an oath I refused,
fearing the words would hasten
my inevitable loss.
I avoided cracks with
halting tiptoe steps in a life or death
game of hopscotch.
My heart tossed ahead.

What She Said

For twenty years, Joe DiMaggio had
two red roses delivered three times
a week to Marilyn Monroe's burial
vault. I wonder if I could have roses
delivered to your grave. What would
the delivery guy's reaction be when
pulling into the little parking lot behind
the Lutheran church in the middle of
the Pennsylvanian woods. Fifth row
down from the top, sixteen spots in.
The commercials on TV and the radio
keep telling me to pick the Mother's Day
gift that would mean the most, to
remember a present for that special
woman in my life, the woman who made
me. Every holiday, manufactured or not,
is the same. I think the perfect gift would
be to stretch myself out on the grass
beside her, close my eyes and let the
dew and time slowly return me to her.
My mother used to tell me that I was the
prettiest girl in the world. I hold my breath
to make it easier to hear her again

Mural

We moved into a new house when
you were six and three.
No longer all in one room,
and a floor away from me,
I painted a mural on your bedroom
wall in order to comfort you.
A hot-air balloon race surrounded
by white clouds in the shapes that we
day dreamed while cuddling together
in our big family bed under the midnight blue
comforter that I held like a tent over us.
You slept inches apart,
talking deep into the night,
and often in the morning I would find you
together in the same bed,
arms and legs akimbo,
but always face to face.

Ode to George Eliot

Please send me flowers even though
I tell you that it's a waste of money.
Read me poems that remind you of me
while we lay in each other's arms,
or better yet, write your own.
Take me to dinner somewhere that
doesn't offer chicken fingers or turkey clubs.
And, if you see a shiny bauble,
I will not turn it down.

Remember me.
Remember me as you pass through
this world and encounter the bluest flower
you have ever seen, bring its memory
home to me.
I want to sit on your tongue,
live behind your eyes.
To be an afterthought is to die the slowest death.

Times Three

It's all for you,
these daily choices,
from the low-fat peanut butter
to the extra health insurance,
all for you,
for you the bins to organize the trains,
the rainbow of colored pencils,
the Spider-Man mittens.
Love makes you read the ingredients
on the label of the baby wipes container,
makes you triple check the front door,
cut the grapes in half.
You make me want to be a better person.
It was in another lifetime,
one of toil and blood,
and it was all for her,
to make her proud.
Now for you,
it's all for you.

In My Cups

I am in my cups, dreaming of lost moments in
an alternative reality where I was worshipped

by the masses, bathed in milk and honey until
my skin was so soft and supple that painters

were laid blind unless looking sideways through
hand mirrors to capture my best side. Champions

came, battling each other through ideas and the
spoken word, to receive the muse's touch.

Instead, I'm eating bulkie rolls out of the bag,
while the travel channel is on in the background.

Our youngest, asleep on the couch next to me,
while I sit here trying to coax out a responsible

simile, is moaning and twisting her lower body
in the afghan, pains in her calves keeping her sleep

restless. Mom used to call them growing pains, my brother wrestled night after night with discomfort.

I have my own, struggling to hunt for my place in this timeline, like a Marvel character shifted to a new

universe. These shoes don't fit, my pants are too tight, and I can't find a decent moisturizer.

One-Two

Sitting in the corner booth at the bar, I am
sipping my watered down screwdriver
through the tiny red straw the local guy
behind the counter put into my drink.
Knowing I'm not from around here, he
gives less than a fuck about customer service.
And knowing that I'm never coming back, I
give less than a fuck about tipping him.
It's an interesting box step that isn't getting
me any closer to forgetting the reason I'm in
the town of my teenagehood, the sort of
place where if you only have a month left to live
you should immediately move to because
that month will now last an eternity.
Another birthday celebrated in the dirt of
your grave. No cake and ice cream or balloons.
We huddled over your stone and discussed
the past year, keeping you abreast of the
traumas and triumphs that you couldn't be
consulted on in person. It never rains while
we're there, but it's pouring now.
I know it's because you miss me, too.

Ticks

We have finite seconds on this rapid sphere,
hurtling each toward our individual nexus.
Doled out in countless minutes to
errands and laundry, sprinkled on
sheets with lovers and bled to dry husks
by jobs who take our best years,
our robust minutes and spend them at
the craps table looking for the six & eight,
while we wash their vomit buckets and
wipe their asses after another night
spent whoring away our twenties and thirties,
and we thank them for two weeks off
in the summer and teach our children
to be grateful for weekends when we
can get more work done.
We daydream about art and our garden,
road trips with friends to farm stands with
strawberries that are so perfect they haunt us.
Then we shuffle with our walkers
on a pilgrimage through the streets of
some European city, whose name
we've chanted for years,
one day I'll, one day I'll, one day I'll.

Acknowledgements

Number Four – originally appeared in *Free State Review*
Atlantic Line – originally appeared in *Yellow Chair Review*
Control – originally appeared in *Open Letters Monthly*
Green Beans – originally appeared in *Iniquity Press*
Dervish, Superstition, Canvas – originally appeared in *Ygdrasil*
Where You Came From – originally appeared in *Change Seven Magazine*
In My Cups, One-Two – originally appeared in *Busted Dharma*
Ticks & This Line Here– originally appeared in *Chiron Review*
Petunias & Immortal – originally appeared in *Nixes Mate Review*
Blockade – originally appeared in *Muddy River Poetry Review*
Some of these poems have appeared in *Pressure Press Presents*

About the Author

Heather Sullivan's poems have appeared or are forthcoming in *Corium, Busted Dharma, Chiron Review, Revolution John, Free State Review, Open Letters Monthly, Street Value, Big Hammer, Barbaric Yawp, Common Ground Review, Nixes Mate Review, Muddy River Poetry Review* and *Trailer Park Quarterly*, among others. She lives near Boston and the ocean, with her charming husband, herds of children and cats, and three beloved whispering trees.

Nixes Mate Books features small-batch artisanal literature, created by writers that use all 26 letters of the alphabet and then some, honing their craft the
time-honored way: one line at a time.

More Nixes Mate titles:
ON BROAD SOUND | Rusty Barnes
KINKY KEEPS THE HOUSE CLEAN | Mari Deweese
SQUALL LINE ON THE HORIZON | Pris Campbell
COMES TO THIS | Jeff Weddle
HITCHHIKING BEATITUDES | Michael McInnis
AIR & OTHER STORIES | Lauren Leja

Forthcoming titles from Nixes Mate:
NIXES MATE REVIEW ANTHOLOGY 2016/17
CAPP ROAD | Matt Borczon
LUBBOCK ELECTRIC | Anne Elezabeth Pluto
A SOUTHERN CHILDHOOD | Pris Campbell
A WORLD WHERE | Paul Brookes
WAR IN THE TIME OF LOVE | Michael McInnis

nixesmate.pub/books

www.ingramcontent.com/pod-product-compliance
Lightning Source LLC
Chambersburg PA
CBHW052135010526
44113CB00036B/2271